EDGE
BOOKS

ORIGAMI
Papertainment

Samurai, Owls,
Ninja Stars, and More!

by Christopher Harbo

CAPSTONE PRESS
a capstone imprint

Edge Books are published by Capstone Press,
1710 Roe Crest Drive, North Mankato, Minnesota 56003
www.capstonepub.com

Library of Congress Cataloging-in-Publication Data
Harbo, Christopher L., author.
  Origami papertainment : Samurai, owls, ninja stars, and more! / by Christopher Harbo.
      pages cm.—(Edge books. Origami paperpalooza)
  Summary: "Provides instructions and photo-illustrated step diagrams for folding a variety
of traditional and original origami models"—Provided by publisher.
  Audience: Ages 8-14.
  Audience: Grades 4 to 6.
  Includes bibliographical references.
  ISBN 978-1-4914-2022-5 (library binding)
  ISBN 978-1-4914-2193-2 (eBook PDF)
1. Origami—Juvenile literature. 2. Handicraft—Juvenile literature. I. Title.
  TT872.5.H377 2015
  736.982—dc23   2014027876

Editorial Credits
Sarah Bennett, designer; Kathy McColley, layout artist; Katy LaVigne, production specialist;
Marcy Morin, scheduler

Photo Credits
All photographs done by Capstone Studio: Karon Dubke

Design Elements: Shutterstock: naihei

Printed in Canada.
102014   008478FRS15

Table of Contents

An Origami Extravaganza   **4**

Materials   **5**

Folding Symbols   **5**

Terms and Techniques   **6**

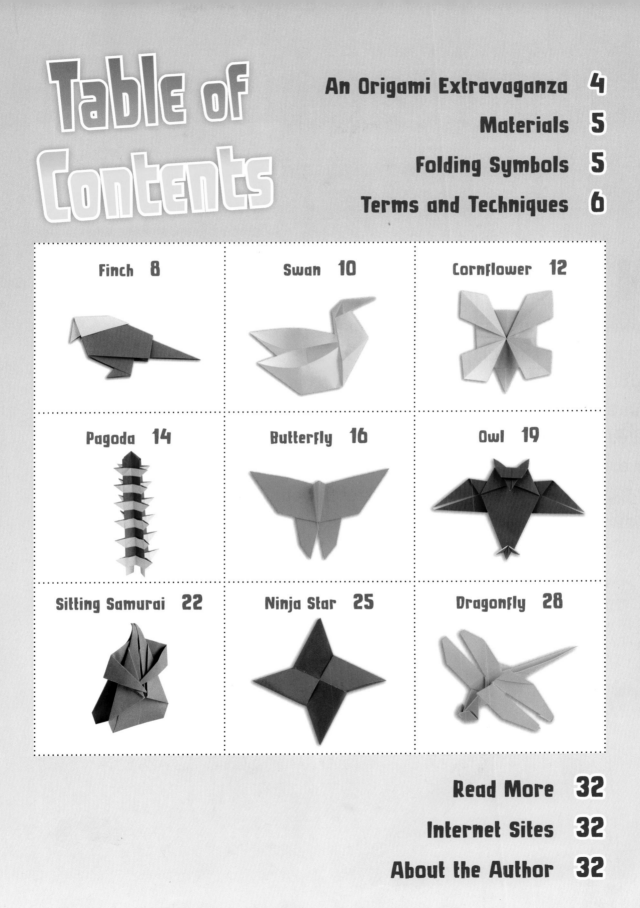

Finch   **8**

Swan   **10**

Cornflower   **12**

Pagoda   **14**

Butterfly   **16**

Owl   **19**

Sitting Samurai   **22**

Ninja Star   **25**

Dragonfly   **28**

Read More   **32**

Internet Sites   **32**

About the Author   **32**

An Origami Extravaganza

Never before has paper been so entertaining! This collection of traditional and original origami models promises hours of folding fun. Amaze your friends by turning two sheets of paper into an awesome ninja star. Build a towering pagoda to serve as a backdrop for a sitting samurai. Decorate your dinner table with paper swans filled with crackers or candies. From finches to cornflowers to dragonflies, these stunning paper creations can be enjoyed in dozens of ways. So stretch your fingers and grab some paper. It's time to start folding!

Materials

Origami is an affordable hobby because it doesn't require many materials to get started. In fact, you'll only need a square sheet of paper for most of the models in this book. A few models may require some extra materials, but you can easily find most of these items around the house:

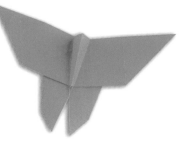

Paper: While you can fold with just about any paper, authentic origami paper often works best. It is perfectly square, easy to fold, and has a crispness that holds its creases well. You'll find packets of origami paper with many fun colors, patterns, and sizes at most craft stores.

Scissors: Sometimes a model needs a snip here or there to pull off a key detail. You won't need it often, but keep a pair of scissors handy.

Ruler: Some models use measurements to complete. A ruler will help you measure.

Paper Trimmer: A good quality paper trimmer will come in handy when you want to cut paper to a custom size. Rotary blade paper trimmers are a good choice for precise, clean cutting. A variety of paper trimmers can be found at any craft store.

Pencil: Use a pencil when you need to mark a spot with the ruler.

Craft Supplies: Markers and other craft supplies will help you decorate your finished models.

Folding Symbols

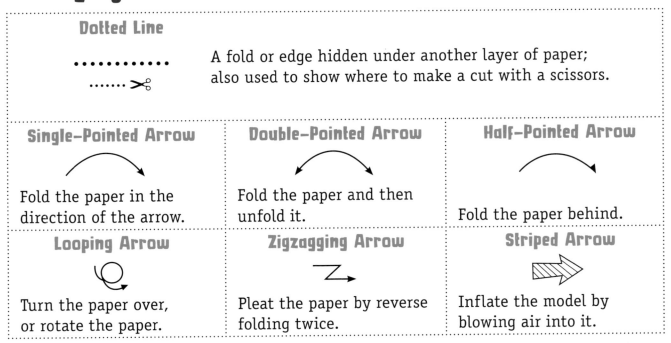

Dotted Line	A fold or edge hidden under another layer of paper; also used to show where to make a cut with a scissors.

Single-Pointed Arrow	**Double-Pointed Arrow**	**Half-Pointed Arrow**
Fold the paper in the direction of the arrow.	Fold the paper and then unfold it.	Fold the paper behind.
Looping Arrow	**Zigzagging Arrow**	**Striped Arrow**
Turn the paper over, or rotate the paper.	Pleat the paper by reverse folding twice.	Inflate the model by blowing air into it.

Terms and Techniques

Folding paper is easier when you understand basic origami folding terms and techniques. Practice the folds below before trying the models in this book. Bookmark these pages so you can refer back to them if you get stuck on a tricky step.

Valley folds are represented by a dashed line. One side of the paper is folded against the other like a book.

Mountain folds are represented by a dashed and dotted line. The paper is folded sharply behind the model.

Squash folds are formed by lifting one edge of a pocket. The pocket gets folded again so the spine gets flattened. The existing fold lines become new edges.

Inside reverse folds are made by opening a pocket slightly. Then you fold the model inside itself along the fold lines or existing creases.

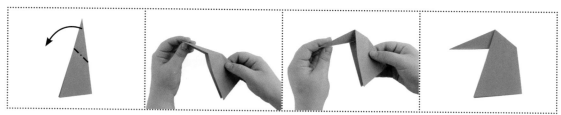

Outside reverse folds are made by opening a pocket slightly. Then you fold the model outside itself along the fold lines or existing creases.

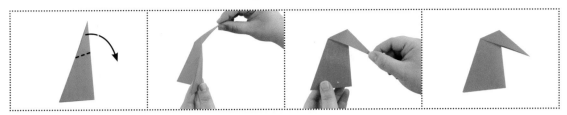

Rabbit ear folds are formed by bringing two edges of a point together using existing fold lines. The new point is folded to one side.

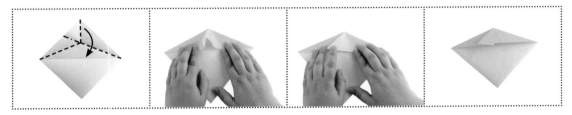

Petal folds are made by pulling a point upward and allowing its sides to come together as the paper flattens.

Pleat folds are made by using both a mountain fold and a valley fold.

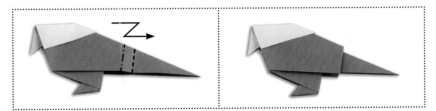

Mark folds are light folds used to make reference creases for a later step. Ideally a mark fold will not be seen in the finished model.

Finch ◆ Traditional

This simple bird resembles the finches often seen hopping around bird feeders. Experiment with double-sided papers to vary the look of your birds.

Tip: A patterned paper that resembles feathers will create finches that mimic nature.

1

Valley fold corner to corner and unfold.

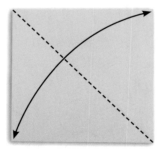

2

Valley fold the edges to the center.

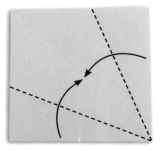

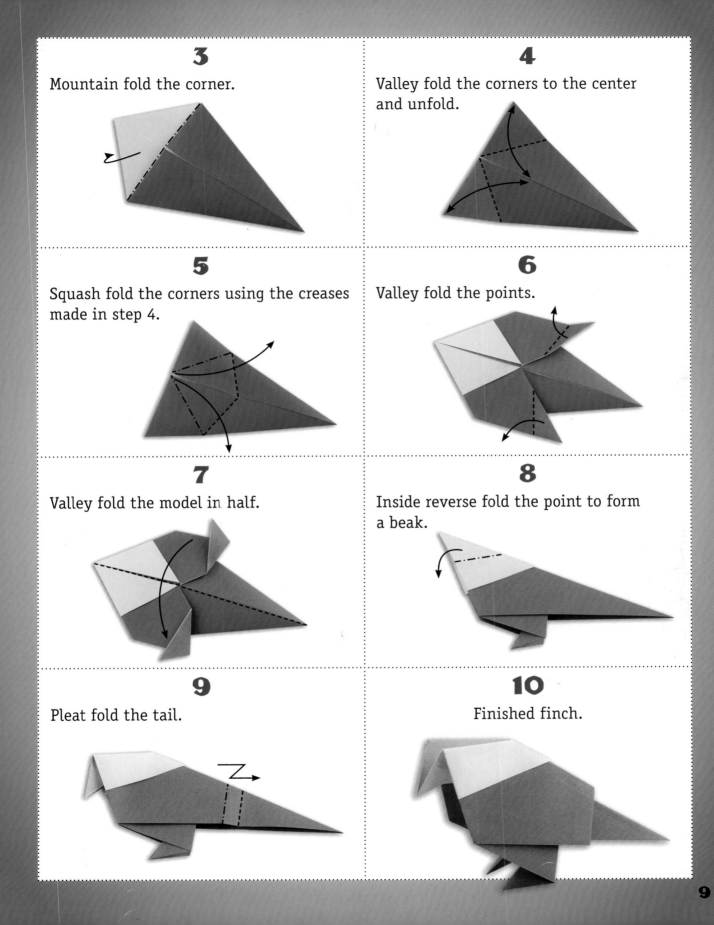

3

Mountain fold the corner.

4

Valley fold the corners to the center and unfold.

5

Squash fold the corners using the creases made in step 4.

6

Valley fold the points.

7

Valley fold the model in half.

8

Inside reverse fold the point to form a beak.

9

Pleat fold the tail.

10

Finished finch.

Swan ◆ Traditional

Decorate the table at your next party with an elegant swan at each place setting. Just puff out its wings to fill them with a colorful assortment of candies.

1

Valley fold corner to corner and unfold. Turn the paper over.

2

Valley fold corner to corner and unfold.

3

Valley fold the edges to the center and unfold.

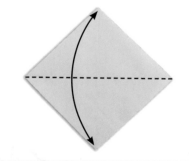

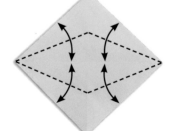

4

Rabbit ear fold on the creases made in step 3. At the same time, mountain fold the center crease.

5

Valley fold both points. Allow the points to land about halfway between the corners and the left point.

6

Valley fold the points.

7

Mountain fold the model in half.

8

Pull the neck up and flatten.

9

Pull the head up and flatten.

10

Mountain fold the bottom point. Repeat behind.

11

Finished swan.

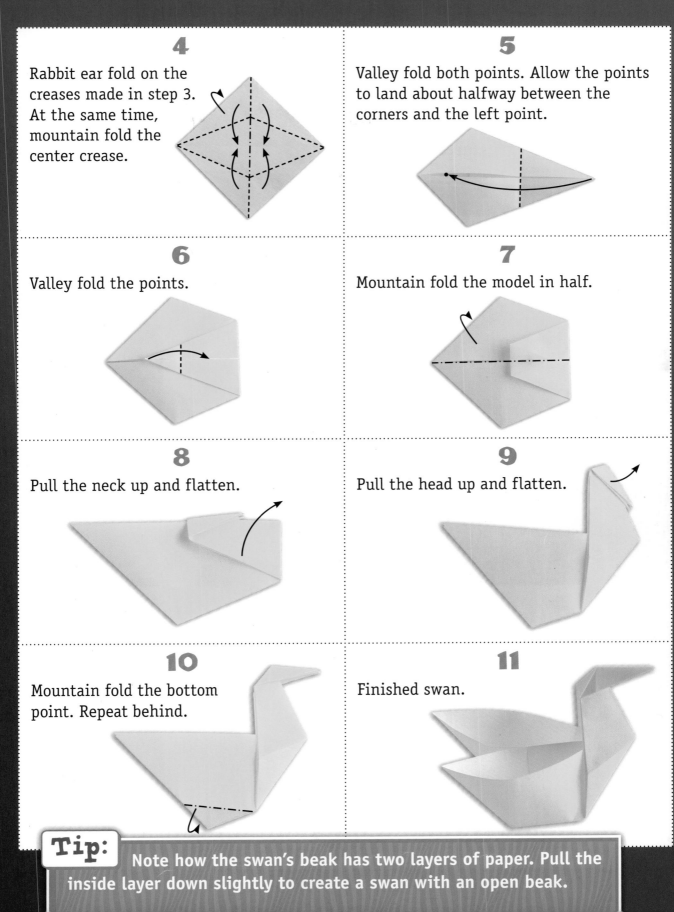

Tip: Note how the swan's beak has two layers of paper. Pull the inside layer down slightly to create a swan with an open beak.

Cornflower ◆ Traditional

Cornflowers burst like stars into brilliant shades of light blue. With four points radiating outward, this origami replica looks great in any color.

1

Valley fold corner to corner in both directions and unfold. Turn the paper over.

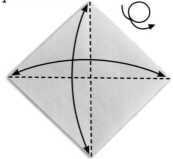

2

Valley fold edge to edge and unfold.

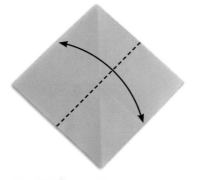

3

Valley fold edge to edge.

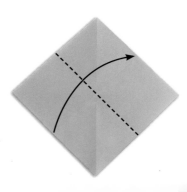

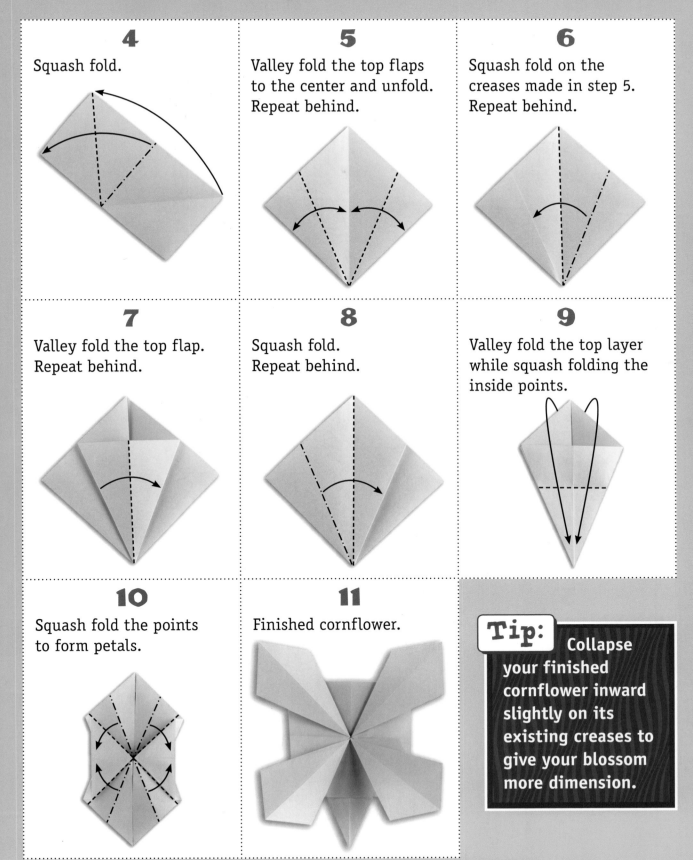

4

Squash fold.

5

Valley fold the top flaps to the center and unfold. Repeat behind.

6

Squash fold on the creases made in step 5. Repeat behind.

7

Valley fold the top flap. Repeat behind.

8

Squash fold. Repeat behind.

9

Valley fold the top layer while squash folding the inside points.

10

Squash fold the points to form petals.

11

Finished cornflower.

Tip: Collapse your finished cornflower inward slightly on its existing creases to give your blossom more dimension.

Pagoda ◆ Traditional

Pagodas are tiered towers found in many countries throughout Asia. This paper pagoda uses multiple pieces of the same model to create one complete tower.

1

Valley fold edge to edge in both directions and unfold. Turn the paper over.

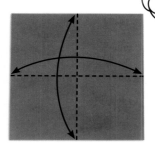

2

Valley fold corner to corner in both directions and unfold.

3

Squash fold the paper using the existing creases.

4

Valley fold the top flaps to the point. Repeat behind.

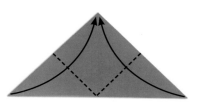

Tip: To enhance the look of your pagoda, use paper with bright colors on both sides.

5

Valley fold the top flaps to the bottom and unfold. Repeat behind.

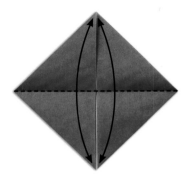

6

Squash fold the top flaps. Repeat behind.

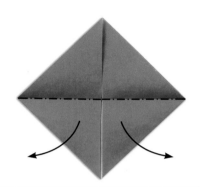

7

Valley fold the top flaps. Repeat behind.

8

Mountain fold the top flaps to the center. Repeat behind.

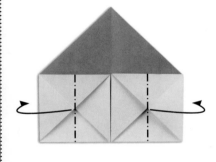

9

Valley fold the point to the center. Repeat behind.

10

Pinch the triangles of the top layer and gently pull outward. Repeat behind.

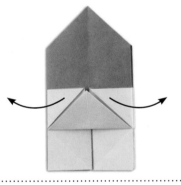

11

Repeat steps 1 to 10 with five more squares. Each square should be cut .25 inch (0.6 centimeter) smaller than the piece before it.

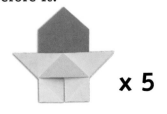 x 5

12

Slide the smaller models on top of the larger models.

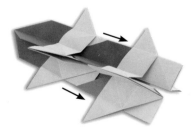

13

Finished pagoda.

Butterfly ◆ Traditional

Butterflies come in countless colors and patterns. Take a hint from nature—let your imagination run wild when selecting colorful paper for this delightful model.

1

Valley fold edge to edge in both directions and unfold.

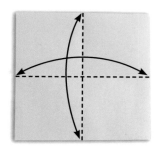

2

Valley fold corner to corner in both directions and unfold.

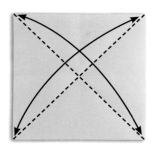

3

Valley fold the corners to the center.

4

Turn the model over.

5

Valley fold the corners to the center and unfold. Turn the model over.

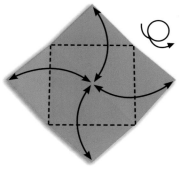

6

Unfold the paper completely.

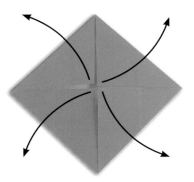

7

Valley fold the edges to the center.

8

Squash fold the corners using the existing creases.

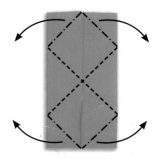

9

Mountain fold the model in half.

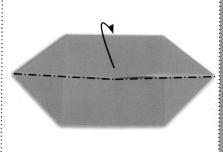

Continued ➡

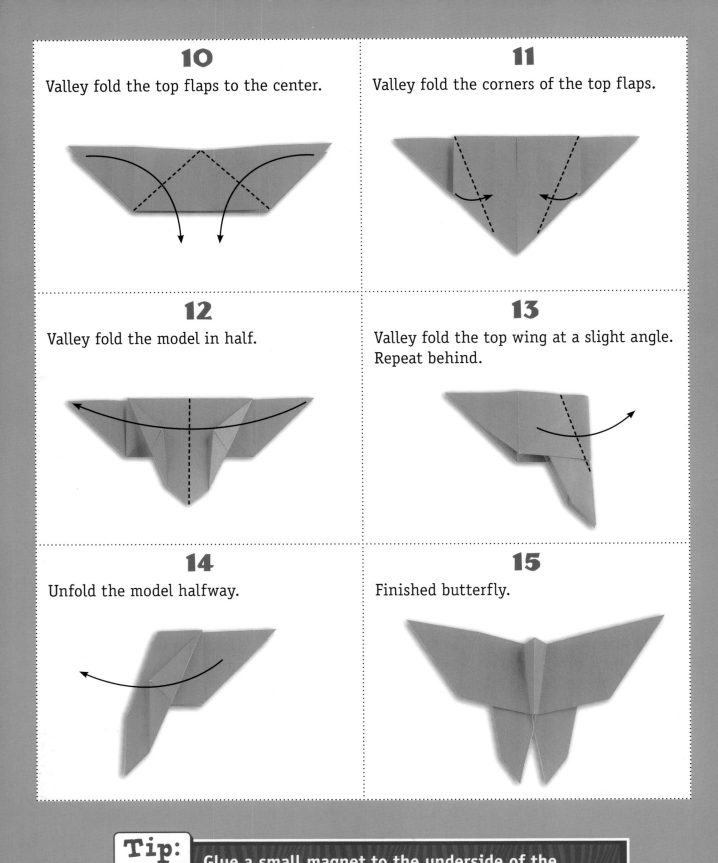

10
Valley fold the top flaps to the center.

11
Valley fold the corners of the top flaps.

12
Valley fold the model in half.

13
Valley fold the top wing at a slight angle. Repeat behind.

14
Unfold the model halfway.

15
Finished butterfly.

Tip: Glue a small magnet to the underside of the butterfly to create an origami refrigerator magnet.

Owl ◆ Traditional

Whoo! Whoo! This wise old owl stretches its wings to show off its magnificent power.

Tip: Try firmly folding down the owl's wings along the angle of the head. Doing so will give it a relaxed, resting pose.

1

Valley fold corner to corner in both directions and unfold. Turn the paper over.

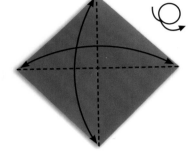

2

Valley fold edge to edge and unfold.

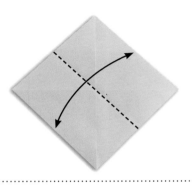

3

Valley fold edge to edge.

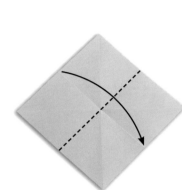

4

Squash fold.

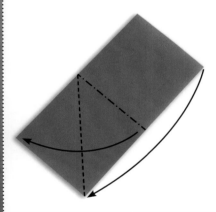

5

Valley fold the top flaps to the center and unfold. Repeat behind.

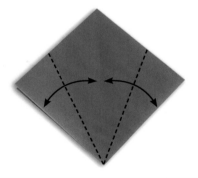

6

Inside reverse fold the top flaps. Repeat behind.

7

Valley fold the top flaps to the center crease. Repeat behind.

8

Lift and twist the hidden center flaps to form the wings.

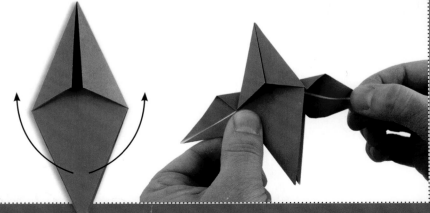

9
Valley fold the point.

10
Valley fold the point.

11
Valley fold to form the head.

12
Turn the model over.

13
Cut the layer of paper on the back of the owl's head. Valley fold the flaps upward.

14
Turn the model over.

15
Cut the bottom point in half. Valley fold the flaps to make feet.

16
Finished owl.

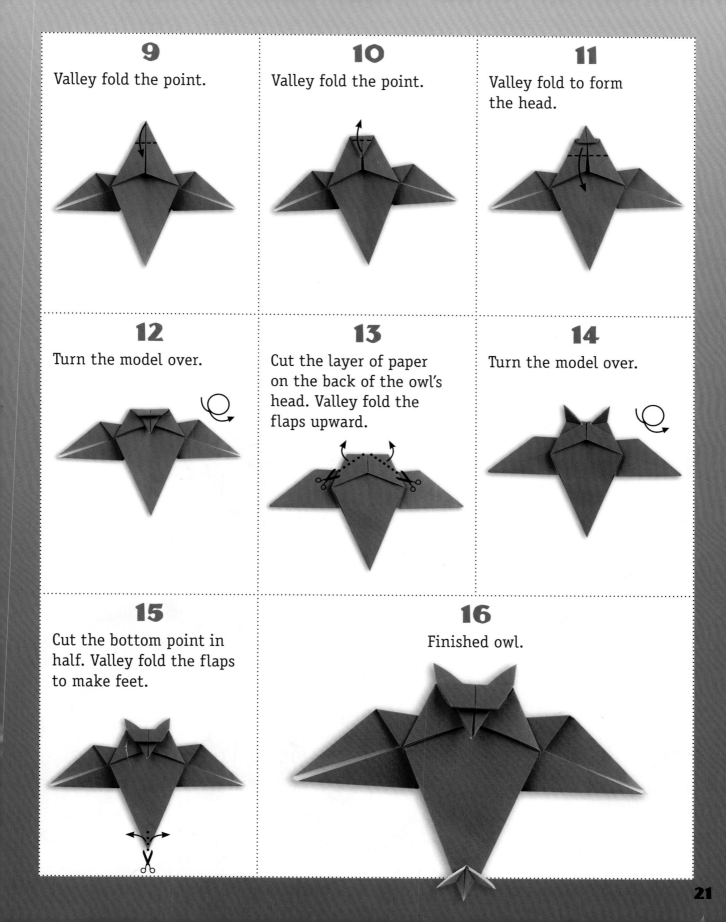

Sitting Samurai ◆ by Christopher Harbo

While samurai were some of Japan's most fearsome warriors, this model imagines a peaceful moment in their lives. With arms folded into the folds of his kimono, this samurai patiently meditates.

Tip: Experiment with patterned paper to bring out the beauty of the samurai's kimono.

1

Valley fold corner to corner in both directions and unfold. Turn the paper over.

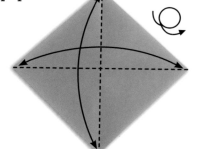

2

Valley fold edge to edge and unfold.

3

Valley fold edge to edge.

4

Squash fold.

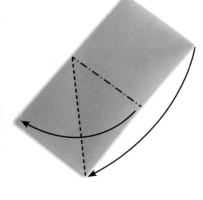

5

Valley fold the top flaps to the center and unfold. Repeat behind.

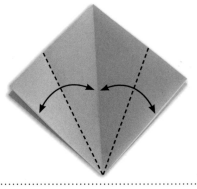

6

Inside reverse fold the top flaps. Repeat behind.

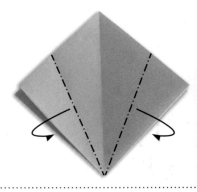

7

Valley fold the top flap. Repeat behind.

8

Valley fold the top flap edges to the center crease and unfold. Repeat behind.

9

Rabbit ear fold on the creases made in step 8. Allow the point to flatten to the right.

10

Turn the model over.

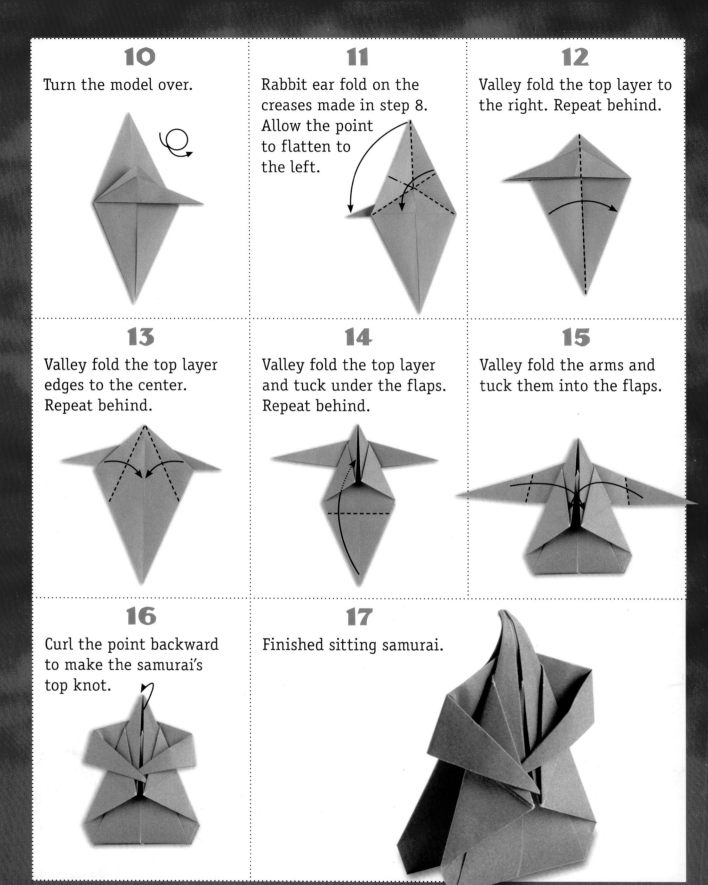

11

Rabbit ear fold on the creases made in step 8. Allow the point to flatten to the left.

12

Valley fold the top layer to the right. Repeat behind.

13

Valley fold the top layer edges to the center. Repeat behind.

14

Valley fold the top layer and tuck under the flaps. Repeat behind.

15

Valley fold the arms and tuck them into the flaps.

16

Curl the point backward to make the samurai's top knot.

17

Finished sitting samurai.

Ninja Star ◆ Traditional

This four-point star resembles the throwing stars, or shuriken, made famous by Japanese ninjas. To tap into your inner ninja, you'll need two pieces of paper.

Tip: Mix solid colors with patterned paper for unique ninja stars.

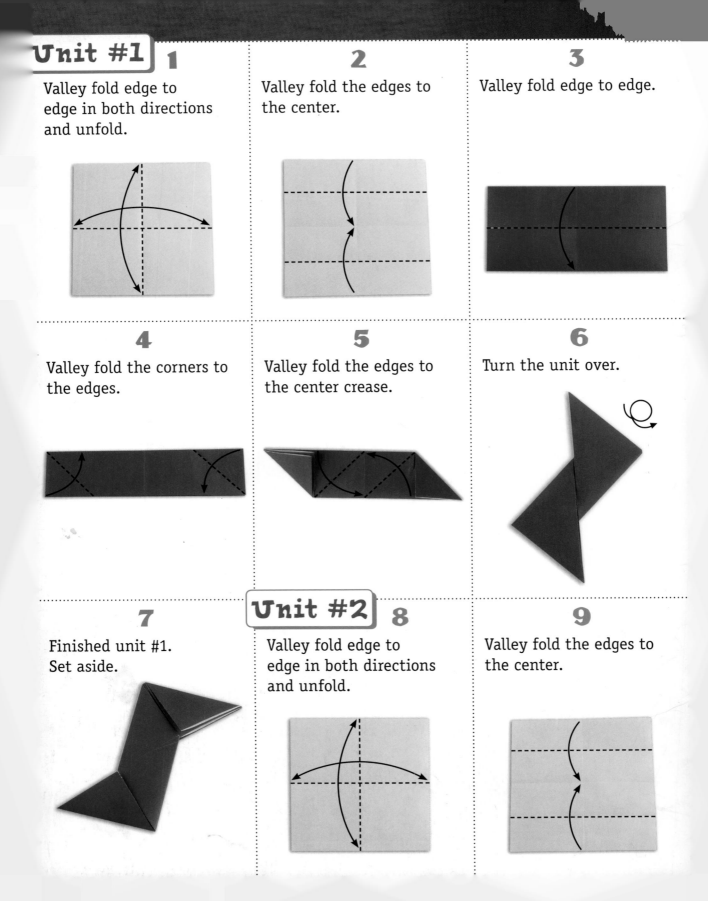

Unit #1

1 Valley fold edge to edge in both directions and unfold.

2 Valley fold the edges to the center.

3 Valley fold edge to edge.

4 Valley fold the corners to the edges.

5 Valley fold the edges to the center crease.

6 Turn the unit over.

7 Finished unit #1. Set aside.

Unit #2

8 Valley fold edge to edge in both directions and unfold.

9 Valley fold the edges to the center.

10
Valley fold edge to edge.

11
Valley fold the corners to the edges.

12
Valley fold the edges to the center crease.

13
Finished unit #2.

14
Lay unit #2 on top of unit #1.

15
Valley fold the points of unit #1 and tuck them into the pockets of unit #2.

16
Turn the model over.

17
Valley fold the points of unit #2 and tuck them into the pockets of unit #1.

18
Finished ninja star.

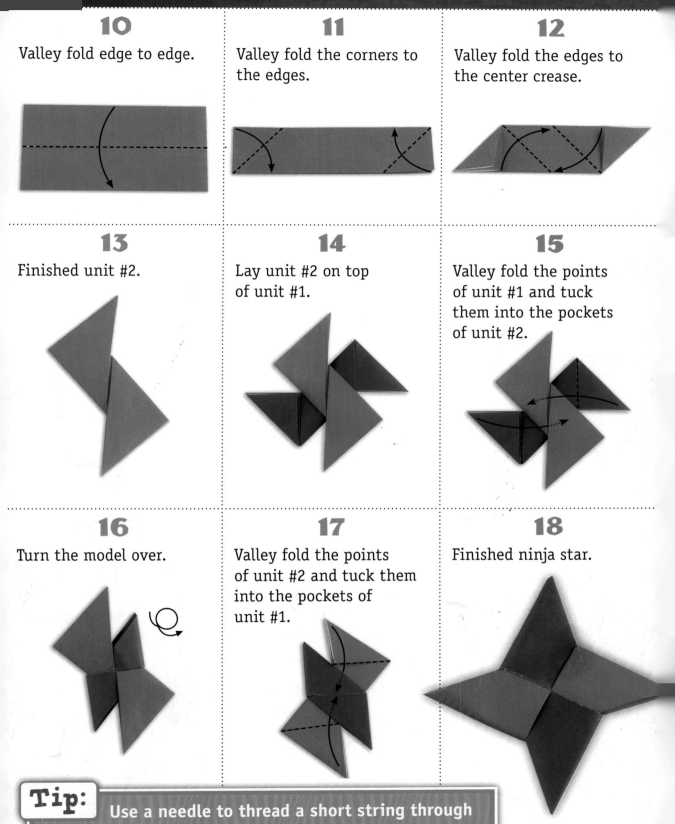

Tip: Use a needle to thread a short string through one point in the star. Then tie the ends of the string together. You've created an instant ornament.

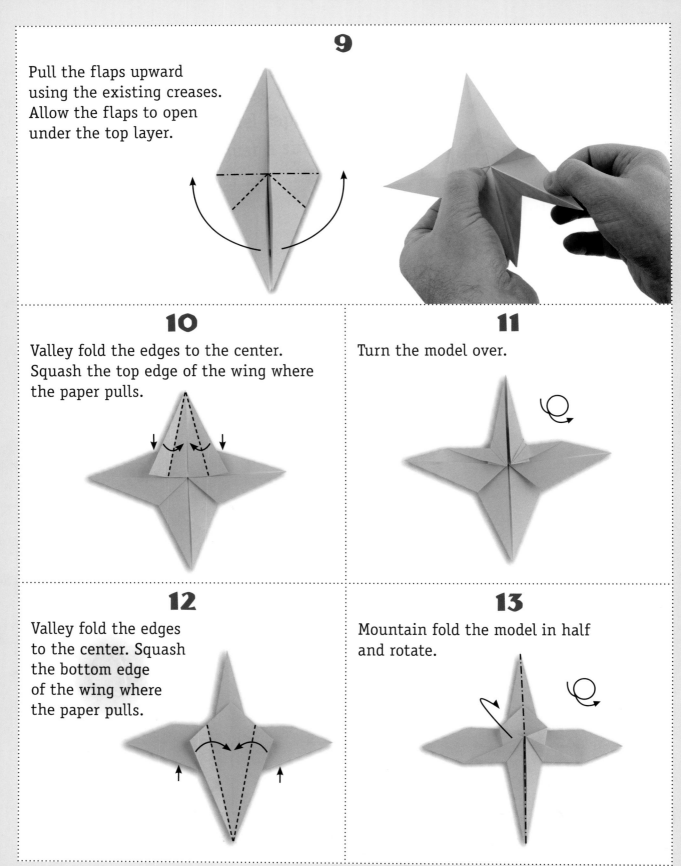

9

Pull the flaps upward using the existing creases. Allow the flaps to open under the top layer.

10

Valley fold the edges to the center. Squash the top edge of the wing where the paper pulls.

11

Turn the model over.

12

Valley fold the edges to the center. Squash the bottom edge of the wing where the paper pulls.

13

Mountain fold the model in half and rotate.

14

Outside reverse fold the point.

15

Outside reverse fold the point five or six times to form the head.

16

Cut the top wing in half. Repeat behind.

17

Inside reverse fold the tips of all four wings.

18

Valley fold the wings halfway. Repeat behind.

19

Finished dragonfly.

Tip: Decorate a flower arrangement or houseplant with origami dragonflies perched on floral wire.

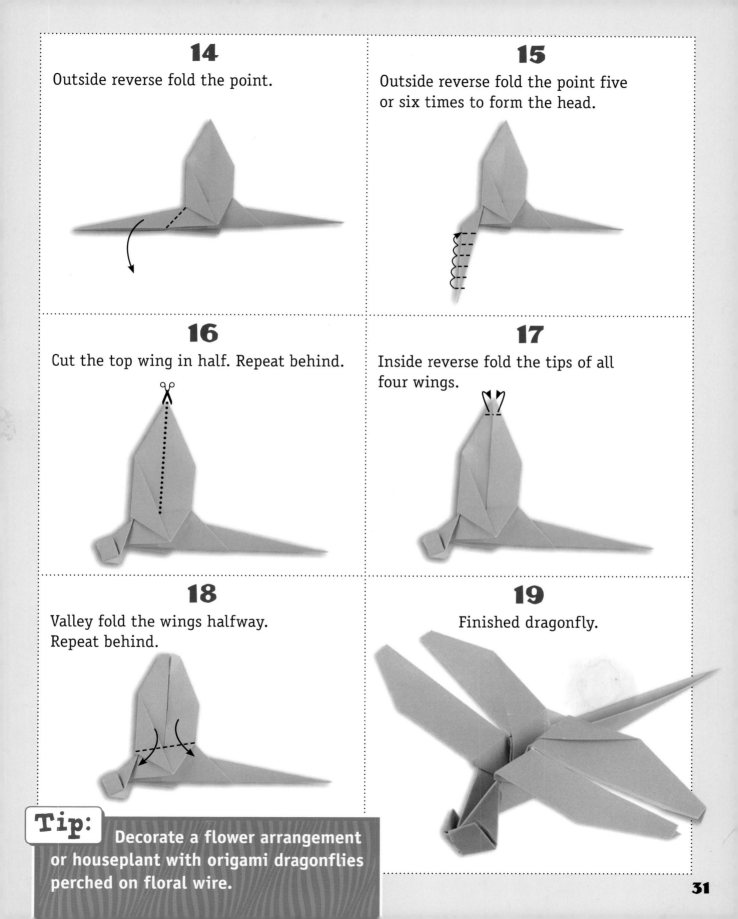

Read More

Bolitho, Mark. *Fold Your Own Origami Army*. Origami Army.
New York: PowerKids Press, 2014.

Miles, Lisa. *Origami Farm Animals*. Amazing Origami.
New York: Gareth Stevens Publishing, 2014.

Montroll, John. *Origami Dinosaurs for Beginners*.
Mineola, N.Y.: Dover Publications, 2013.

Internet Sites

FactHound offers a safe, fun way to find Internet sites related to this book. All of the sites on FactHound have been researched by our staff.

Here's all you do:
Visit *www.facthound.com*
Type in this code: 9781491420225

Check out projects, games and lots more at
www.capstonekids.com

About the Author

Christopher Harbo has a passion for origami. He began folding paper 10 years ago when he tried making a simple model for his nephews. With that first successful creation, he quickly became hooked on the art form. He ran to his local library and checked out every origami book he could find to increase his folding skills. Today he continues to develop his origami skills and loves the thrill of folding new creations. In addition to traditional origami and its many uses, he also enjoys folding paper airplanes and modular origami. When he's not folding paper, Christopher spends his free time reading Japanese manga and watching movies.